Away in a Manger
Violin Sheet Music

Arr. Aaron Chase

James Murray

Away in a Manger
Violin Sheet Music

Arr. Aaron Chase

James Murray

Come, Thou Long Expected Jesus

Arranged for Violin

Arr. Aaron Chase

Charles Wesley

COME, THOU LONG EXPECTED JESUS
Arranged for Violin

Arr. Aaron Chase

Charles Wesley

God Rest You Merry, Gentlemen
Violin Sheet Music

Arr. Aaron Chase

English Melody

God Rest You Merry, Gentlemen

Violin Sheet Music

Arr. Aaron Chase

English Melody

Good Christian Men, Rejoice

Violin Sheet Music

Arr. Aaron Chase

German melody, 14th cent.

Good Christian Men, Rejoice
Violin Sheet Music

Arr. Aaron Chase

German melody, 14th cent.

Hark! the Herald Angels Sing

Arranged for Violin

Arr. Aaron Chase

Mendelssohn

Rit... (last time through).

Hark! the Herald Angels Sing

Arranged for Violin

Arr. Aaron Chase

Mendelssohn

Rit... (last time through).

It Came upon the Midnight Clear

Violin Sheet Music

Arr. Aaron Chase

Richard S. Willis

It Came upon the Midnight Clear
Violin Sheet Music

Arr. Aaron Chase

Richard S. Willis

Joy to the World! The Lord Is Come
Violin Sheet Music

Arr. Aaron Chase

Handel

Joy to the World! The Lord Is Come
Violin Sheet Music

Arr. Aaron Chase

Handel

O Come, All Ye Faithful
Violin Sheet Music

Arr. Aaron Chase

JOHN FRANCIS WADE

O Come, All Ye Faithful

Violin Sheet Music

Arr. Aaron Chase

John Francis Wade

O COME, O COME, EMMANUEL

Violin Sheet Music

Arr. Aaron Chase

PLAINSONG

O Come, O Come, Emmanuel

Violin Sheet Music

Arr. Aaron Chase

PLAINSONG

O Little Town of Bethlehem
Violin Sheet Music

Arr. Aaron Chase

Lewis H. Redner

O Little Town of Bethlehem

Violin Sheet Music

Arr. Aaron Chase

Lewis H. Redner

Silent Night! Holy Night!
Violin Sheet Music

Arr. Aaron Chase

Franz Gruber

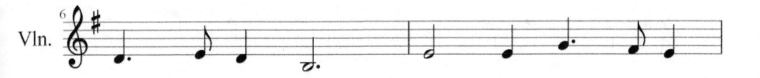

Silent Night! Holy Night!

Violin Sheet Music

Arr. Aaron Chase

FRANZ GRUBER

What Child Is This?

Violin Sheet Music

Arr. Aaron Chase

English Melody

What Child Is This?

Violin Sheet Music

Arr. Aaron Chase

English Melody

CPSIA information can be obtained
at www.ICGtesting.com
Printed in the USA
LVOW05s1711251116

514319LV00032B/143/P

9 781494 928315